Freedom of Expression

Deal with it

before you are CENSORED

Danielle S. McLaughlin • Illustrated by Paris Alleyne

James Lorimer & Company Ltd., Publishers
Toronto

You are in a bad mood.

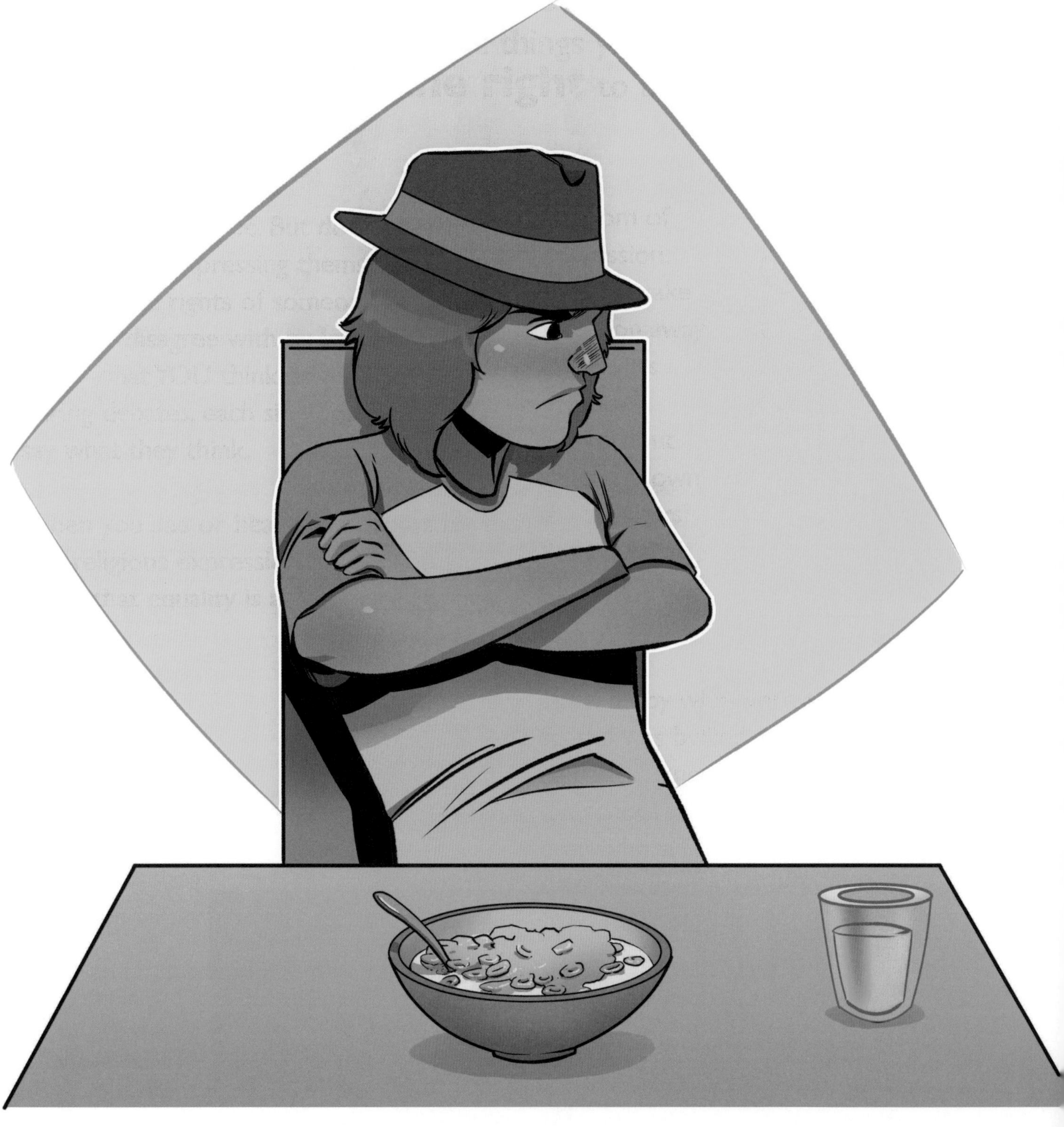

You put on your hat and stomp downstairs to the kitchen. Your grandma tells you to take your hat off and sit down. You yell that you hate your hair and want to wear the hat all day. You are not going to take it off — ever. Your grandma tells you it is rude to wear a hat indoors — and your school has a no-hats rule. "So off it comes!" she says.

Can you express yourself any way you choose? Can everyone?

What does it mean to have freedom of expression? Should there be limits to what people can say or do to express themselves?

This book will help you to explore the ins and outs of freedom of expression. You will find there are many places where our freedoms are limited by laws, by rules and regulations, as well as by customs such as good manners. Is that fair? Read on and decide for yourself.

Contents

What is Freedom of

Every person is born with the right to be who they are, to be free, to be safe, and to express themselves. One of your rights is called freedom of speech. But it's really freedom of *expression* because you communicate in many ways, not just by speaking.

Most of us understand that we have the right to:

- Speak our minds
- Dress the way we want
- Listen to our favourite music
- Write down our ideas and thoughts
- Post what we think and do online and on social media
- Read any book or magazine we choose
- Perform in any play or concert we please
- Paint or draw anything we can imagine

Expression?

But, should you:

- Go topless to school?
- Write swear words on someone's locker?
- Publish a school blog that calls your principal nasty names?
- Post a recipe for making a stink bomb?
- Play a hip-hop song with lyrics that insult and threaten girls on the school's PA system?
- Post a "Who is the ugliest kid?" contest on social media?

When you express yourself, other people might disagree with you. When one person's rights get in the way of someone else's, conflict can happen.

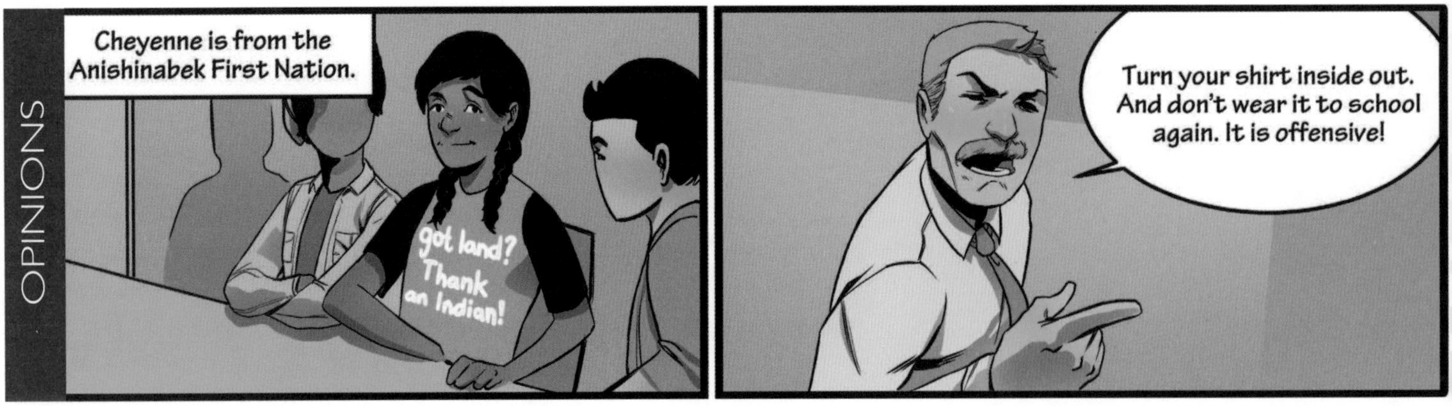
OPINIONS
Cheyenne is from the Anishinabek First Nation.
got land? Thank an Indian!
Turn your shirt inside out. And don't wear it to school again. It is offensive!

Freedom of expression

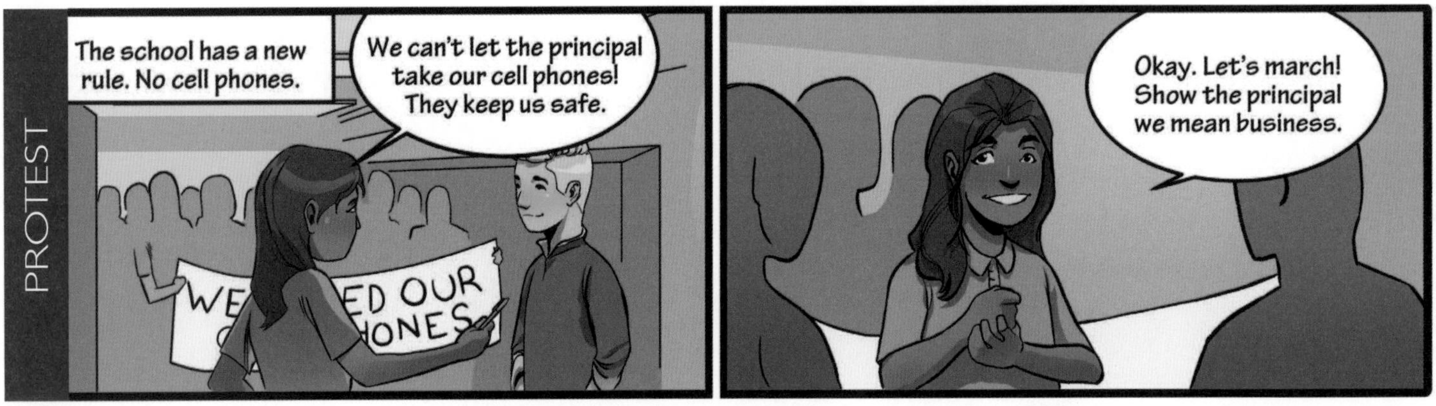
PROTEST
The school has a new rule. No cell phones.
We can't let the principal take our cell phones! They keep us safe.
Okay. Let's march! Show the principal we mean business.

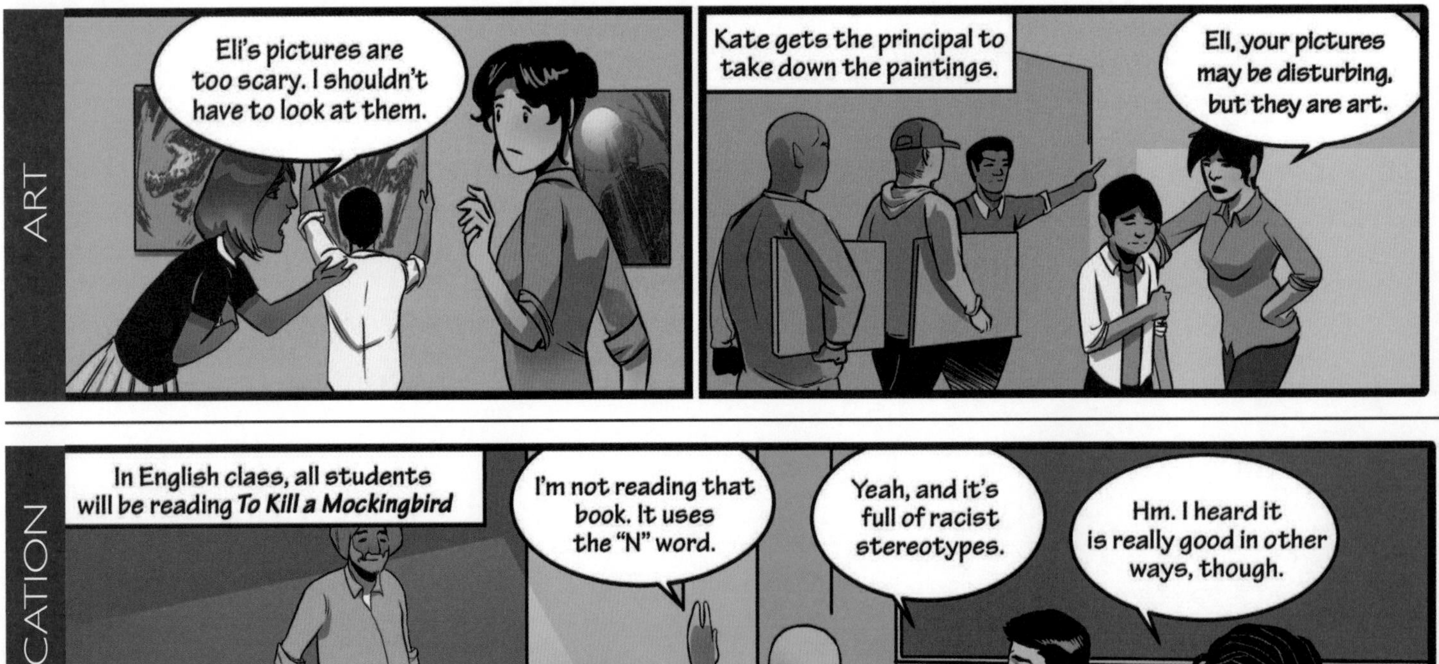
ART
Eli's pictures are too scary. I shouldn't have to look at them.
Kate gets the principal to take down the paintings.
Eli, your pictures may be disturbing, but they are art.

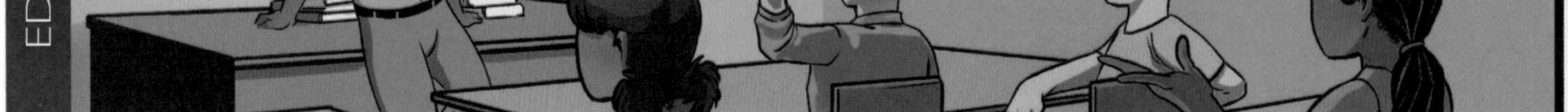
EDUCATION
In English class, all students will be reading *To Kill a Mockingbird*
I'm not reading that book. It uses the "N" word.
Yeah, and it's full of racist stereotypes.
Hm. I heard it is really good in other ways, though.

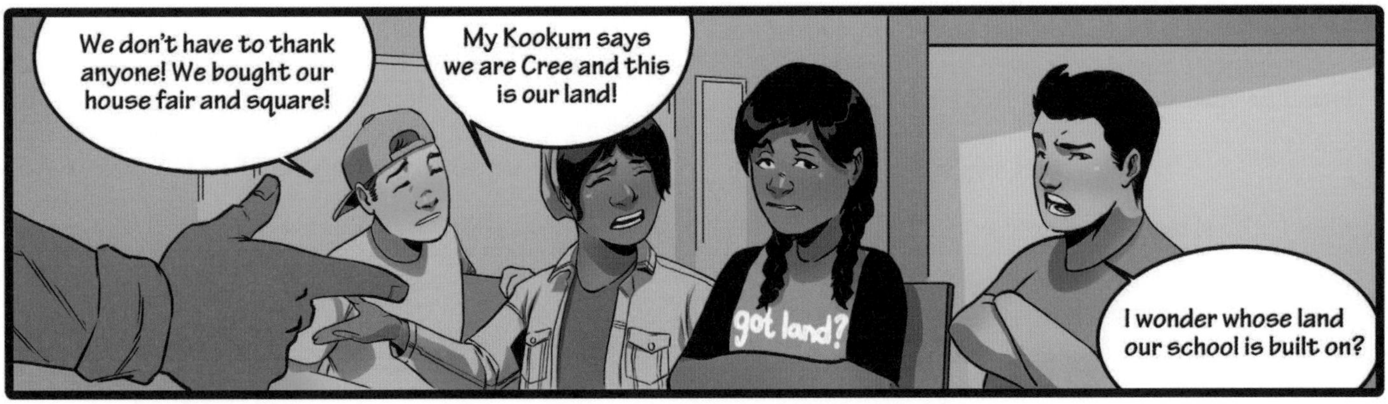
We don't have to thank anyone! We bought our house fair and square!
My Kookum says we are Cree and this is our land!
got land?
I wonder whose land our school is built on?

can protect...

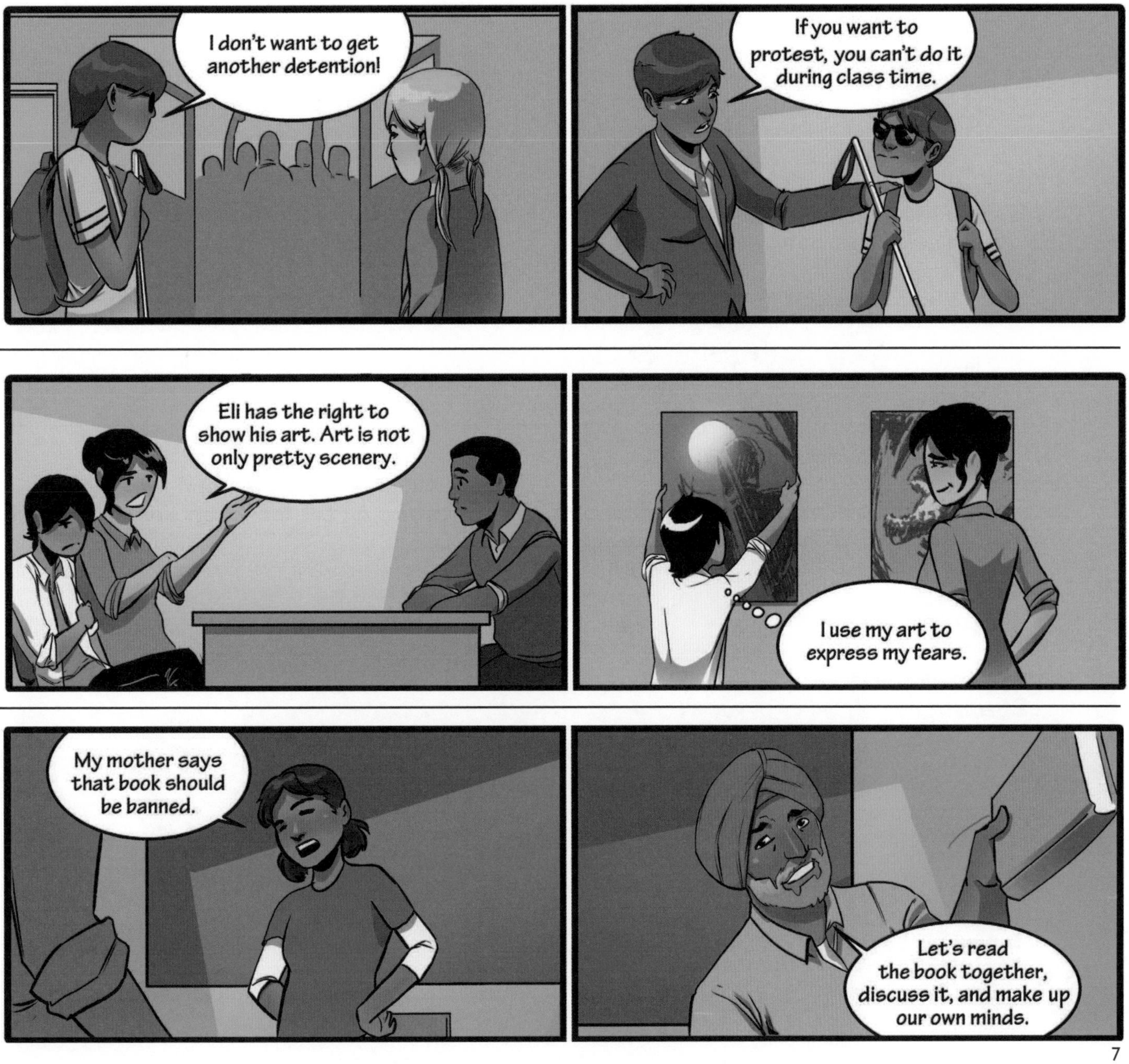
I don't want to get another detention!
If you want to protest, you can't do it during class time.
Eli has the right to show his art. Art is not only pretty scenery.
I use my art to express my fears.
My mother says that book should be banned.
Let's read the book together, discuss it, and make up our own minds.

QUIZ

Censorship or Not?

Censorship is the opposite of freedom of expression. If rules keep us from expressing our views without a good reason, that could be unfair. But sometimes, we need to know when and where to express ourselves — it's just good manners. So, is it censorship or not?

1 Stop the Noise!

Your mother tells you to turn your music down. It is too loud for her.

Not censorship. Your mother is trying to get the family to live in harmony!

2 Bulletin Bored

Student Bulletin Board

Your school has a new rule. Nothing can be posted on the student bulletin board without the principal's approval.

This is called "prior restraint." It is a kind of censorship.

3 Read the Wall

You are caught writing "Black Lives Matter" in the washroom. The teacher makes you wash the graffiti from the wall.

Not censorship. You don't get to vandalize school property.

4 'Tis the Season

The principal announces that the school Christmas concert will now be called the winter concert and take place in January.

Not censorship. The principal is not keeping anyone from celebrating Christmas.

5 Fiesta Faceoff

You and your family are celebrating Cinco de Mayo with music, dancing, and great food. You ask your next-door neighbour to come join the party, but he tells you to go away. He thinks Mexican festivals don't belong in this country.

Not censorship. Everyone can ask people to go away from their homes, no matter the reason.

⑥ Hip-Hop Cop

You and your friends are dancing to hip hop in a public park. A police officer says the words to your songs are offensive. She says she will arrest you if you don't stop.

The police can move you along if you are blocking traffic. But it is **censorship** if police tell you what lyrics you can't sing or listen to.

⑦ Video No-No

At the public library, you notice that the man at the next computer has a sex video on his screen. When you report it to the librarian, she tells the man to leave.

Not censorship, since it is in a public space.

⑧ Halt the Hate

The word "terrorist" is sprayed on a mosque, a Muslim house of worship. Down the street, the police arrest a person holding a can of spray paint.

Not censorship. No one can deface another's property, and this could be a hate crime.

⑨ Book Ban

The public school's librarian decides to remove all books by gay authors.

This is censorship, even though you can get the books from other places.

⑩ Bible Backdown

The local church wants to distribute Bibles to all the kids in your school. Your principal says they can't use the school for this purpose.

Not censorship. Public schools cannot promote any one religion.

Freedom of Expression 101

Dear Conflict Counsellor

Q: In geography class, our teacher told us the earth is flat. He gave our class a new book that he says proves it. Is he allowed to do that?
— *Wanting a Well-rounded Education*

A: Your teacher is required to teach what is in the curriculum, not his own theories. All your approved textbooks will tell you that the earth is shaped like a ball. This teacher can believe that the earth is flat, and he can tell you that there are non-scientists who think this. But he cannot teach it as an "alternative fact" if it goes against the curriculum.

Q: I go to a school where we have to wear uniforms. I say this is unfair because it stops me using fashion to express myself.

— *Fashionisto*

A: Before your family signed you up at your school, they were told that everyone must wear a uniform. While it might not have been your choice, your parents decided against a school with no uniforms. Just so you know, some schools have dropped their uniform rule when enough parents and students protested.

Q: I saw a man downtown last Sunday. He was telling everyone that they are going to hell if they don't follow his beliefs and practices. I was really upset by what he said. Can I get the police to arrest him?

— *Call the Cops*

A: I am sorry you were upset by the preacher on the street. But it is not against the law to offend or upset people. So police won't arrest him. But there are things you can do if you don't like what he is saying. Can you think of ways you could use your free speech to counter his? You could ask to talk to him and then tell him why you think he is wrong. Also, if he can stand there telling people what to believe, so can you! You can even write and hand out pamphlets or make a sign telling people what you think.

Q: Sometimes I see things on social media that are not true. I saw someone famous accused of a crime it turns out they didn't commit. What happens when someone tells lies about another person?

— *Stop the Gossip*

A: Sometimes, nothing happens. But a person who is falsely accused can go to civil court to sue the liar for libel (if they lied in writing) or slander (if spoken). If the falsely accused person can prove that the lies hurt their reputation, the liar could end up paying a lot of money.

Myths !!!

It is against the law to use racist words.

It is not against the law, but it is a rude and offensive thing to do. You can lose a lot of friends this way.

I can say anything I want to.

There are many reasons why certain kinds of expression is not allowed. For example, you can't shout "Fire!" in a crowded theatre — unless there really IS a fire, of course! That's because it could cause a stampede and people could get hurt.

Teachers have the same right to freedom of expression as everyone else.

Teachers are supposed to be role models. They could lose their jobs for saying or doing certain things. For example, teachers have been fired for posting pictures of themselves drunk or in the nude.

DID YOU KNOW?

• Some high school students in Toronto petitioned and got rid of their dress code.

It is against the law to say bad things about people.

It is usually not a crime to say bad things. But it is an awful thing to do.

Protesting and using our free speech to complain never changes anything.

If you live in a country where citizens can vote and you have rights, it's because of freedom of speech. You can thank protesters who used their freedom of expression to fight oppression and make your country what it is.

THE FUTURE IS FEMALE

Kids can go to jail for being rude to their teachers.

In most countries, if you are under twelve, you can't be sent to jail at all. But being rude to your teachers can still get you into trouble at school and with your family.

- In the US, students cannot be suspended for peaceful political protest in school.

- Freedom of the press is an important part of freedom of expression.

- Winnie the Pooh was once banned because some people said talking animals offended their religion.

The **Censor**

Does it really bug you when friends complain that the rules aren't fair? Do you want to ban music with rude words or movies about issues that make you uncomfortable? Do you wish there was some way of keeping your friends from wearing clothes that are "so last year"? What can you do when no one seems as nice as you or has the same good taste you have?

DEAR DR. SHRINK-WRAPPED...

Q: I learned in school that people of Japanese descent were forced to go into camps or were deported to Japan during World War II. It makes me feel awful to hear about this. Can I get the school to stop teaching about this bad time in Canadian history?
— *Sad Student*

A: It sounds like you are sensitive to the suffering of other people, Sad. That is a great place to start understanding history. But feeling sad is not a good reason to stop learning. We all need to learn about what happened in the past because it helps us to understand our mistakes — and then we can avoid making them again. Yes, the Canadian and US governments caused many bad things to happen to Japanese-Canadians and Japanese-Americans before and during World War II. But the inclusion of people of Japanese descent has given both countries writers, artists, business people, scientists, teachers, and so many others. Ask your teacher if she can help you find books to read about how Canada apologized for treating Japanese-Canadians and their families in such a terrible way.

dos and don'ts

✓ Do respect other people's views and opinions.

✓ Do take the time to listen to views that are unpopular.

✓ Do feel free to leave a movie or a concert that upsets you.

✓ Do use your words to let others know what you think.

✓ Do understand that complaining can be the first step to making changes.

✓ Do let your friends and family be themselves.

✓ Do ask an adult for help if you feel threatened.

✓ Do keep calm when you hear or read offensive expressions.

✗ Don't make snap judgments about someone else's views.

✗ Don't assume that everyone needs to look the same or believe the same things you do.

✗ Don't feel bad if you decide to walk away from someone who is offensive.

✗ Don't feel you have to correct everyone's views.

✗ Don't always run away from disagreements.

✗ Don't think that banning words will stop ideas from existing.

✗ Don't be afraid to say what you think.

✗ Don't think adults are always right.

✗ Don't think censorship will make hatred go away.

QUIZ

Are you a control freak?

Do you really hate hearing or seeing anything that people could disagree about? Do you think nobody should be allowed to say anything that is offensive or might hurt someone's feelings? Take this quiz to see what you can find out about yourself.

Of the following statements, how many are true and how many false?

1. I think people should always be polite.

2. Graffiti is always vandalism.

3. I could never stand up for the rights of someone who disagrees with me.

4. I think art should only show pretty images.

5. I hate debates.

6. It is dangerous to let people disagree because it could start a fight.

7. Books that make some people uncomfortable should be banned from the library.

8. Teachers should not be allowed to talk about same-sex families.

9. Teachers should not tell students their personal views.

10. People who can't vote should not be allowed to protest.

11. I don't think controversial topics belong in school.

12 I don't want to read anything with bad words.

 13 I won't be seen with friends who wear things I find embarrassing.

 14 I don't think people should be allowed to kiss in public.

 15 You should never talk about your political opinions on social media.

 16 Protests don't change anything.

 17 No one should say "Merry Christmas" because it could offend people who aren't Christian.

 18 Music and movies that have sex and violence shouldn't be allowed.

 19 Banning hate speech makes people safe.

 20 People should be arrested for telling racist jokes.

 21 No one should be allowed to challenge my thinking.

 22 Evolution should not be taught in biology class.

 23 Books that are really offensive should be burned.

 24 Comedians who use bad language don't belong on TV or YouTube.

 25 Someone needs to control what stories the media can report.

If you answered **TRUE** **to a lot** of these statements, you might need to go back and think about **why** we have **freedom of expression.** Try to imagine what would happen if your right to be treated fairly were **taken away. Without freedom of expression,** how could you do anything about it?

Freedom might depend on you!

It would be nice if everyone could **just agree** about how the world should be. **But they don't.** Rules or demands that everyone be the same could keep you from **standing up** for your own rights. There are basic things you can do to make sure that **everyone has the right** to be who they are — including **you**.

Feel free to disagree. But don't prevent others from expressing themselves. Support the rights of someone whose side you disagree with by letting people know what YOU think as well. Just like during debates, each side needs time to say what they think.

When you see or hear racist, sexist, or anti-religious expression, let the speaker know that equality is as important as

freedom of expression. Can you take attention away from ideas you don't like without shutting down the speakers? Some kids in Nova Scotia started Pink Shirt Day when a boy who wore a pink shirt to school was bullied and called homophobic names. The next day, nearly everyone in the school wore pink shirts. Now, students everywhere fight bullying and celebrate their freedom of expression by wearing pink shirts on a special day each year.

DID YOU KNOW?

- *Where's Waldo* was banned in 1987 when someone saw a bare breast in a crowded beach scene.

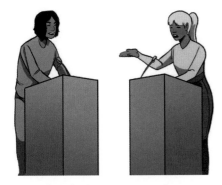

You don't have to take everything you see or hear seriously. There are cartoons that make fun of serious subjects and comedians who poke fun at people in power. Sometimes the best response to views you dislike is to laugh at them and help others see how absurd those views are.

Some schools have debating teams or clubs. They help students learn how to disagree respectfully on controversial topics. If your school doesn't have a team, you could start one. Find people with very different views, bring them together, and make them think!

When Obscenity Is Involved

Our governments protect people's right to express themselves. But many countries have laws against obscenity. What does that mean? "Obscenity" usually refers to pictures, words, and videos that have to do with sex and/or violence that many people find disturbing and offensive. But because different people have different tastes, and because values change over time, the idea of what is obscene keeps changing too:

- It was once "obscene" for women to show their ankles or the backs of their necks.
- Some famous pop stars have been arrested and banned for obscenity because they used "dirty words" in their songs.
- Nude statues once had to have their genitals covered with fig leaves.
- In the 1950s, you couldn't say the word "pregnant" on TV.

When You See Something

If you are offended by something you think is obscene:

- Remember that not everyone feels the way you do.
- Tell a trusted adult what you saw or read. Then you can discuss it and decide what to do next.
- Use your right to leave a movie, block social media, turn off music, or look away from images you don't like.
- If you believe a real person was harmed in the making of a video or photograph, you can report it to the police.

When You Want to Express Something

What if you're an artist, musician, writer, or video maker? What if you plan to be one someday? You could be worried about including something obscene or getting into trouble for something you create.

Remember that not everyone will like what you do.

Some artists use their work to shock their audiences. This is okay. But if you cross the line of what is "socially acceptable," you should be ready for people to complain or try to stop you.

What is thought to be obscene will depend on the creator and the audience — on who they are, and when and where their work appears.

- Cartoon character Tweety Bird used to be pink. When people complained he looked naked, they made him yellow.

- In the 1920s, some people tried to ban saxophone music because they thought it was too sexy. They called it "the devil's flute."

The **Speechmaker**

Nobody can accuse you of being too shy to express yourself.

You stand up and say what you want, whenever you want. You wear what you like and post your views on social media for the world to see.

But freedom of expression **is not an absolute right.** We all have to decide where and when to draw the line.

DEAR DR. SHRINK-WRAPPED...

Q: My friends and I love hip-hop music. Sometimes we pretend to be our favourite music group and sing their songs out loud. One of the songs uses the "N" word a lot. My friends and I identify as being from all different races. We usually just belt out that word, but one of my friends told me she is uncomfortable using it. Don't we have the right to sing whatever we want?

— Lil' Me

A: Dr. Shrink-Wrapped loves singing along, too. But only in the shower. Legally, you can use any words you like, no matter how you identify, Lil'. But if your friend doesn't want to sing the "N" word, you should respect how she feels. Talk with your group and support your friend in explaining how she feels. See if you can find songs that everyone enjoys singing — including all the words. Or you can all just sing along, with each person skipping the words they don't want to use or making up new ones. It's up to you! And there is always the shower.

dos and don'ts

✓ Do enjoy peaceful disagreements.

✓ Do choose a safe time to speak up.

✓ Do keep an open mind when you hear different opinions.

✓ Do remember that you don't have to believe everything you read or hear.

✓ Do feel free to tell people what you think.

✓ Do let an adult know if you feel threatened or afraid.

✓ Do know your facts. If it sounds like a lie, it might well be a lie.

✓ Do pick your battles. Some arguments are not worth it.

✗ Don't try to control the opinions of people around you.

✗ Don't feel bad if you disagree with a friend or family member.

✗ Don't feel you need to always stand up for everyone's rights — sometimes you need a break.

✗ Don't use violence to show your disagreement.

✗ Don't deface or destroy property.

✗ Don't be afraid to use your creativity to get attention for your ideas.

✗ Don't forget to learn from people who are different from you.

QUIZ

Are you thoughtful when you express yourself, or do you go too far?

Where do you draw the line? When someone challenges you, you can oppose them, back down, or talk about it. Take this quiz, then check your answers on the opposite page to see how you are doing.

I Oppose Them

I Back Down

I Talk About It

1 School Slam

The principal is sick of the student newspaper reporting bad things about the school. She makes a rule that anyone who writes a story that shows the school in a bad light will be suspended. You just wrote a story for the paper about the broken toilets in the girls' washrooms. What should you do?

a) Throw the story away and write one about the new garden instead.

b) Ask the principal about her plans to repair the school.

c) Tell the principal that when the plumbing gets fixed, you will write a story about that.

a) back down   b) talk   c) oppose

---

2 Complaint Department

Katrina is always complaining. She is the first one to find a problem and then won't stop talking about it. Your friends are getting tired of all the complaints and want you to do something about it. What should you do?

a) Ignore it. That's just Katrina's way.

b) Tell Katrina that if she can't find something nice to say, she shouldn't say anything at all.

c) Ask Katrina if there is a reason she is so negative and unhappy.

a) back down   b) oppose   c) talk

---

3 Dress for Success

You have joined a new community centre that has a rule: everyone must wear "appropriate attire" to use the gym. But your religion requires you to wear ankle-length dresses, not the gym clothes other people wear. What should you do?

a) Just wear dresses to the gym anyway.

b) Go to the community centre manager and explain that the rule is limiting some people's freedom of expression.

c) Quit the gym and find another way to exercise.

a) oppose   b) talk   c) back down

---

4 Doesn't Add Up

Math is your favourite subject, but your new math teacher suggested that you avoid algebra because Black kids aren't good at math. What should you do?

a) Tell the teacher about famous Black mathematicians and ask him to look at your work.

b) Tell the principal that the math teacher is prejudiced.

c) Wait to do algebra until next year, when you have a different teacher.

a) talk   b) oppose   c) back down

---

5 Club Controversy

Your friends have just started a Vietnamese club at your school. You want to be with your friends, but you are not Vietnamese. What should you do?

a) Tell the principal you don't think this type of club should be allowed.

b) Forget the club and see your friends at other times.

c) Ask your friends to let you join the club so you can learn to speak Vietnamese, too.

a) oppose   b) back down   c) talk

---

6 Pronoun Problem

As a transgender person, you prefer that people use the pronouns they, their, and them for you. Your English teacher says that is bad grammar and refuses to use these words the way you have asked her to. What should you do?

a) Rudely ignore the English teacher when she uses the wrong pronoun.

b) Talk to the teacher to explain how the English language has changed over time.

c) Ask to transfer to a different school.

a) oppose   b) talk   c) back down

---

7 Lizard Lessons

You found out that your teacher, Ms. Kartofle, believes that lizard people secretly rule the world. In fact, she has a blog about it. Because she only teaches gym, the subject doesn't come up at school. What should you do?

a) Say nothing because some teachers are just weird.

b) Tell your parents to complain to the school and transfer you to a different gym teacher's class.

c) Give Ms. Kartofle some books written by scientists.

a) back down   b) oppose   c) talk

---

8 Party Rule

Your school has a rule against wearing "offensive" messages on clothing. Your favourite T-shirt has a picture of Che Guevara on it. Your teacher says that she is offended because she believes communism is evil and her family fled Cuba after the communist revolution. What should you do?

a) Stand up and tell the teacher you think Che is a hero.

b) Turn the shirt inside out and only wear it on weekends.

c) Talk to the teacher about including different political beliefs in classroom discussions.

a) oppose   b) back down   c) talk

---

9 Bathing Beauty

Your best friend posted a picture of you in a bathing suit on Instagram. The photo attracted lots of nasty comments about your appearance. What should you do?

a) Decide never to look at Instagram again.

b) Talk to your friends about posting kind comments on Instagram photos they see.

c) Tell your friend you never want to speak to them again.

a) back down   b) talk   c) oppose

---

10 History Lesson

A guest speaker in your class talks about residential schools, where Indigenous children were taken from their families, often abused, and forced to attend for years at a time. You are shocked to hear the speaker say that residential schools were not as bad as everyone says, and that the stories of abuse are exaggerated. What should you do?

a) Yell at the speaker that she is wrong and start a loud argument.

b) Quietly leave the room while the guest speaker is talking.

c) Ask your family and the principal to talk to the teacher about what the class is learning.

a) oppose   b) back down   c) talk

The **Speechmaker**

There are times when standing up and speaking out might not be such a good idea. Being responsible means making thoughtful choices.

Don't let them get to you.

Some people say nasty things just to draw attention to themselves. You don't have to engage with them, especially if you feel unsafe doing so. You can walk away.

Think before you speak.

Your right to express your views doesn't mean you should be nasty to people. Something you think is a joke or a good story might make you seem mean and prejudiced. Think about what your words and actions say about you.

Get organized.

Your right to join peaceful groups and your freedom of expression can be powerful tools in the fight against prejudice. A single voice is easy to ignore. But if you and a few hundred of your closest friends get together to protest, people will listen. The best answer to bad speech is MORE speech, not censorship.

DID YOU KNOW?

- It's a crime to deny the Nazi Holocaust in several European countries.

When Hate Is Involved

Even though the law protects our right to freedom of expression, problems can arise when one person's rights conflict with another's.

Hate Crime

Freedom of expression can include our actions. But hate crime is different from hate speech. A hate crime is a criminal act that is based on or made worse by hate.

- Beating up a person is a crime. Beating them up because they are gay is a hate crime.
- Toppling gravestones is a crime. Toppling gravestones in a Jewish cemetery and spray painting them with Nazi swastikas is a hate crime.
- Breaking windows is a crime. Breaking windows in a mosque to show anti-Islamic feeling is a hate crime.

Hate Speech

Where they exist, laws against hate speech are complicated. Even lawyers can have trouble understanding them.

In Canada, it is illegal to express hate against certain groups of people just for being that group — usually a specific race, religion, or gender identity — if the words or images are likely to lead to a "breach of the peace." That means you can't use "fighting words" in public that will lead to people being hurt. Breaking this law could land a person in jail.

Just saying something horrible about a group of people is not likely to be considered hate speech. But it can depend on who is speaking and where and when they choose to deliver their nasty messages.

By the way, anything a friend or a family member shares with you in private, even if what they say is racist or prejudiced, is not illegal. But feel free to challenge what they say. Remind them that just because they have the right to say ugly things, it doesn't mean they should!

Remember that you are not alone.

Sometimes it is difficult to tell the difference between expression that is offensive and expression that is dangerous. If you feel that anyone's safety is being threatened, tell a teacher, an adult family member — or the police. No one has the right to threaten or harm anyone.

- Cartoonists were murdered for drawing pictures of the Prophet Muhammad.

- There are no laws in the US against hate speech, but you can't use "fighting words" that lead to people getting hurt.

You don't like to offend people.

It hurts your feelings when you hear remarks that are racist, sexist, homophobic, transphobic, or prejudiced against any religion.
But you also know that freedom of expression is important in the fight against these ugly ideas.
You don't want to restrain rights. But what can you do when you witness that kind of prejudice?

Be a Freedom Fighter

When you are speaking out, organizing against censorship, calming down your friends, or just telling someone what you think, you are a champion. And champions make a difference. When you draw attention to a problem, even in a small way, you are showing people that freedom of expression matters. You are fighting for fairness and keeping the path clear for democracy!

Safety First

Sometimes it's just too challenging to stand up for the rights of people who say awful things. That's okay. You don't have to be fighting the fight every day. You need to decide when it's safe to speak out, when to get help, and when to walk away. You also need to let your friends know what you really believe. That way, they can be inspired by what a champion you are!

dos and don'ts

✓ Do learn the facts. You can't fight against lies without knowing the truth.

✓ Do tell people who say racist, sexist, and homophobic things that you don't agree with them.

✓ Do speak up online and in real life when you see an injustice.

✓ Do find ways to be creative.

✓ Do keep safe.

✗ Don't lose your sense of humour.

✗ Don't confuse standing up for freedom of expression with agreeing with everything you read or hear.

✗ Don't be afraid to get help from organizations that specialize in fighting for rights.

✗ Don't think all opinions are equally acceptable.

✗ Don't go near people who use violence as a form of expression.

✗ Don't be afraid to draw attention to yourself.

✗ Don't think burying disagreement makes it go away.

✗ Don't give up. It might take a long time to fight for freedom, but if you don't do it, who will?

The **Witness**

QUIZ

It can be hard to know what to do when everyone is exercising their freedom of expression. Sometimes there is no perfect way to react. But you do have choices! Each of these situations has several possible options — and no answer is right or wrong. You might even come up with a different solution that works for you.

2 ## Going, Going, Gone

Your friend Jo loves old movies. She wants you to sit with her to watch *Gone with the Wind*. She says it is a classic, but you feel uncomfortable because of the way it shows Black people as slaves. What should you do?

- Keep quiet and watch the movie.
- Tell Jo you would rather watch a newer movie.
- Suggest that the two of you watch an anti-racist movie.
- Let Jo know why the movie upsets you.
- Explain to Jo that you will be interrupting to point out why some scenes are racist.

1 Language Barrier

Your best friend speaks Mandarin at home and with her other Mandarin-speaking friends. Since you speak only English and French, it sometimes makes you feel left out. What should you do?

- Spend less time with your friend when she is with her Mandarin-speaking friends.
- Just ignore them when they speak Mandarin.
- Ask your friend politely if she and the others could speak English or French when you are with them.
- Tell your friend that you understand it is important for her to practise her Mandarin, but it hurts your feelings when you are not included in their group.
- Sign up for Mandarin classes.

3 Magic Spell

Your uncle is always putting down what people are reading. You love the Harry Potter books and so does your little brother. Your uncle told you that you must be devil worshippers to believe in magic. What should you do?

- Ignore your uncle.
- Ask your uncle where he got his ideas about the Harry Potter books.
- Encourage your brother to read whatever he likes.
- Tell your uncle that a lot of people read the Harry Potter books and are not devil worshippers.
- Ask your uncle if he has ever read a Harry Potter book. If he hasn't, offer to lend him your copy to read.

4 Hair-y Problem

Your supply teacher told Dakota, a boy in your class, to get a haircut. You know that Dakota belongs to a First Nations community and is growing his hair long for a special ceremony. What should you do?

- Tell Dakota to ignore the supply teacher.
- Offer to help Dakota stand up for himself.
- Tell the teacher that how people wear their hair is one of the ways they express themselves.
- Ask Dakota if he wants you to go with him to the office to report that he is being treated unfairly by the supply teacher.

5 T-Shirt Trouble

Katie is a religious girl in your school. She is always trying to tell the other kids what they should believe. Today she is wearing a T-shirt that says, "Life Without Jesus Is Not Worth Living." What should you do?

- Just ignore the T-shirt. Maybe it is the only clean one she has to wear.
- Ask Katie about her religion.
- Tell Katie that she can believe what she wants, but you believe something different.
- Get together with your friends and buy Katie a different T-shirt.

Continues . . .

6 **Bare-ly Dressed**

You have a favourite music star who performs wearing very little clothing. You have several of her posters in your room, but your family tells you to take them down. What should you do?

- Talk with your family about why the posters upset them.
- Move the posters to a place where your family can't see them, like inside your closet.
- Tell your family that this is how performers dress to express who they are.
- Ask your family not to come into your room if they are going to impose their views on your decorating.
- Talk to your parents about the things you admire about the singer other than her clothing.

7 **Photo Bomb**

A kid in your school likes to take photos when people don't see him doing it. Last week he took one from down below while a teacher in a skirt was walking up stairs. He posted the photo on social media and now everyone can see her underwear. What should you do?

- Just ignore it. No one needs to look at the post.
- Ask the teacher if she knows about the picture. If not, show it to her.
- Tell the kid that he is invading the teacher's privacy and ask him to take the picture down.
- Go to the office and ask the principal to handle it.

DID YOU KNOW?

- Several kids' books about puberty have been banned or removed from public libraries.

8 Talking Terrorism

Some kids you know are talking about terrorism. Silas says his father hates Muslims because they are all terrorists. He shows everyone a website that he believes proves it. What should you do?

- Tell Silas that terrorists can be from any religion, race, or nationality.
- Get a book about Islam from the library to show him what Muslims really believe.
- Ask the teacher to invite a Muslim speaker to tell the class about Muslim life and religion.
- Show the anti-Muslim website to the teacher and ask the school to deal with it.

9 Threat of Violence

Someone has written Shanice's name and the words "Let's get her" on the school washroom mirror. What should you do?

- Ask Shanice if you can help her deal with the threat.
- Go with Shanice to tell a teacher, the principal, and her family about the threat.
- Take some paper towels and rub off the words.
- If you think you know who wrote it, tell the people in the office.

10 Cattle Call

Two animal rights protesters dressed in cow costumes are in the schoolyard. They are handing out stickers and booklets that say milk is poison. They are telling kids never to drink milk or eat meat because it hurts animals. What should you do?

- Ignore the protesters.
- Ask the protesters why they believe what they are saying.
- Tell your teacher or your family that you are confused about whether to drink milk and eat meat anymore. Find out what they think about it.
- If you think the protesters are wrong, organize a counter-protest across the street. Serve chocolate milk!

- In the 1970s, protesters were arrested in Toronto for waving "Yankee Go Home" signs.

- Indigenous children in residential schools were punished for speaking their home languages.

More Help

Each of us needs to express who we are, but only you know what feels right for you in different situations. Learning where and when to speak up for rights takes time and critical thinking. Whatever you choose to do or say, remember that your safety and that of others is most important.

If you want more information or need to talk about your thoughts and ideas, the following resources might help.

Help Organizations

Kids Help Phone 1-800-668-6868

Justice for Children and Youth 1-866-999-JFCY

Anti-Hate Hotline, B'nai Brith 1-800-892-2624

B.C. Civil Liberties Association 1-866-731-7507

National Council of Canadian Muslims 1-866-524-0004

LGBT Youth Line 1-800-268-9688

Websites

American Civil Liberties Union www.aclu.org (US resource)

Article 19 www.article19.org

The Ontario Justice Education Network www.ojen.ca

That's Not Fair! videos, games, and teacher resources www.thatsnotfair.ca

Canadian Civil Liberties Education Trust www.ccla.org/education

EGALE Canada www.egale.ca and www.mygsa.ca

UNICEF Canada www.unicef.ca/en/childrens-rights-0

Youth for Human Rights www.youthforhumanrights.org/what-are-human-rights/universal-declaration-of-human-rights/articles-1-15.html

Kids' Books

A Portrait of the Artist as a Young Lobster: The Right to Speak, Sing, and Laugh, Dustin Milligan and Meredith Luce, DC Canada Education Publishing, 2012

How to Build Your Own Country, Valerie Wyatt and Fred Rix, Kids Can Press, 2009

That's Not Fair! Getting to Know Your Rights and Freedoms, Danielle S. McLaughlin and Dharmali Patel, Kids Can Press, 2016

Naked Mole Rat Gets Dressed, Mo Willems, Hyperion, 2009

For Hooley, my most beloved fellow warrior for freedom of expression.

Copyright © 2019 by Danielle S. McLaughlin
Illustrations © 2019 by Paris Alleyne

Published in Canada in 2019.
Published in the United States in 2019.

James Lorimer & Company Ltd., Publishers acknowledges funding support from the Ontario Arts Council (OAC), an agency of the Government of Ontario. We acknowledge the support of the Canada Council for the Arts, which last year invested $153 million to bring the arts to Canadians throughout the country. This project has been made possible in part by the Government of Canada and with the support of Ontario Creates.

Series design: Blair Kerrigan/Glyphics
Cover design: Tyler Cleroux
Cover image: iStock

Library and Archives Canada Cataloguing in Publication

McLaughlin, Danielle S., 1951-, author
        Freedom of expression : deal with it before you are censored / Danielle S. McLaughlin ; illustrated by Paris Alleyne.

(Deal with it)
ISBN 978-1-4594-1393-1 (hardcover)

        1. Freedom of expression--Juvenile literature. 2. Freedom of speech-- Juvenile literature. 3. Censorship--Juvenile literature. 4. Freedom of expression--Miscellanea--Juvenile literature. 5. Freedom of speech-- Miscellanea--Juvenile literature. 6. Censorship- Miscellanea--Juvenile literature. I. Alleyne, Paris, illustrator II. Title. III. Title: Deal with it before you are censored. IV. Series: Deal with it (Toronto, Ont.)

JC585.M46 2019   j323.44   C2018-905306-2

James Lorimer & Company Ltd., Publishers
117 Peter Street, Suite 304
Toronto, ON, Canada, M5V 0M3
www.lorimer.ca

Distributed in Canada by:
Formac Lorimer Books
5502 Atlantic Street
Halifax, NS, Canada
B3H 1G4

Distributed in the US by:
Lerner Publisher Services
1251 Washington Ave. N.
Minneapolis, MN, USA
55401
www.lernerbooks.com

Printed and bound in China.
Job #: 815150